In Search of a Right-Brained Computer

In Search of a Right Brained Computer

The Story

Let me tell you a story …

I love computers. I think the way they do, i.e. very left-brained. My wife, well let me put it this way, does not have a love affair with computers. Sure, she can use computers, she used to program mainframes in FORTRAN using punch cards. If you don't know what mainframes or FORTRAN or punch cards are, don't worry about it – I can guarantee that you'll never have to know. Just suffice it to say, that those terms refer to heavy duty computer use. So, why doesn't she love computers? They don't think the way she does, which is very right-brained.

On a scale of 1 to 10, with 10 being the highest, when it comes to being left-brained, I'm a 6, but I can be a 10 if I have to. When it comes to being right-brained, my wife is also a 6, and I'm certain she could lean towards a 10 if she wanted to. So, we're not extremely left-brained or right-brained, except from each other's perspective.

Since I love computers, I'd like my wife to love computers or at least not get so frustrated with them. So, for the past 30+ years, I've been searching for a computer she could love. But since all computers and computer systems are designed by left-brained people, I've come up short.

I might have been dissuaded me from my pursuit of the elusive right-brained computer, but my love for her, keeps me going.

So, what is a right-brained computer? In order to answer that question, imagine for a moment that you're looking to buy a computer. What would you look for? What would sway you to buy one computer over another?

In Search of a Right Brained Computer

First: What's its story? If you're left-brained, a computer's story tends to be its current state. Its current state can be told by its features. That is, the operating system (Windows, Android, Linux, iOS, MacOS), the amount of memory, the speed, etc. In other words, "What makes this puppy fly?"

If you're right-brained, the story tends to be its history and purpose. In other words, "How did it get to be this way, and what can it be used to accomplish?" or "… and what will it be in a future rendition?"

Second: How do I use it? If you're left-brained, that translates to, "How do I control it?"

If you're right-brained, the gist is more, "What does it do for me?" This may be stated as "How can we work together?", "Can we be friends?", "How easy is it to use?". A right-brained person may think of this as, "How simple is it to use? And if it's not simple, how much am I willing to change my life to figure it out?"

Third: How does it interact with my senses – sight, sound, smell, and touch? Using the sense of sight, us lefties would say, "How does it look?" Righties might say, "What does it look like?" Lefties are looking for a description that probably includes dimensions. Righties are looking for a description that describes the appearance – what does it go with, how will it blend in or stand out?

Fourth: What is its value? This is a matter of cost versus worth.

Left-brained people tend to think in a straight-line, from start to end. Hmmm, I think I just flunked being left-brained ☺. Right-brained people tend to think circularly – there is no start or end. Left-brained people tend to be more technical, right-brained people tend to be more functional. Left-brained people tend to think in words. Right-brained people tend to

In Search of a Right Brained Computer

think in pictures. Left-brained people tend to look at the world as being static. Right-brained people tend to look at the world as being flexible.

> *Both left-brained and right-brained thinking are valid — neither is better; though we all tend to think that our way of thinking is the best.*

Fifth: What is its life? Is it durable (left-brained)? Is it sustainable (right-brained)? Durable would be, is it sturdy? How long will it last? Sustainable would be how easily can I upgrade it to a newer model? Can it be recycled? Can it be reused – turned into some other useful thing?

This question can be stated as, "What is its lifetime?" (left-brained) versus "What is its legacy?" (right-brained).

Sixth: How does it communicate versus how does it help me communicate? Or, how do I share information (left-brained) versus how do I share my life (right-brained)?

In Search of a Right Brained Computer

> *As you can see, many of these questions could be stated the same for both left-brained and right-brained people. But they would be interpreted totally differently by each group.*

Seventh: How badly do I need or want this? Left-brained people tend to evaluate what they need or want this for – which may be to make them cool. Right-brained people tend to ask, "How will this make me complete?" which may also be a form of cool.

In Search of a Right Brained Computer

> *Left-brained people tend to talk using explanations, discussions, debate, and reasoning.*
>
> *Right-brained people tend to talk using stories, metaphors, analogies, and illustrations.*

So, what were those questions you might ask about a computer you were thinking of buying?

Questions	Left-Brained	Right-Brained
Story	Present-State	History & Purpose
Usability	Control	What does it do for me?
Sensory	Look	Appearance
Value	Cost	Worth
Life	Lifetime	Legacy
Communication	Information	Life
Need/Want	I need this for	This makes me complete

In Search of a Right Brained Computer

That's a left-brained explanation. For a right-brained explanation, read this chapter (again).

While a person may tend to look at life from either a left-brained or a right-brained perspective, most people are neither totally left-brained or right-brained, and do from time to time look at life from the other perspective and from both perspectives. And some people my be left-brained for some of the questions, yet right-brained for others.

And, not everybody asks all those questions all the time.

> *The ultimate computer would be one that appeals to and worked in both perspectives — both left-brained and right-brained.*

In Search of a Right Brained Computer

Whew! All that left-brained/right-brained stuff was exhausting. Time for a little diversion!

Virtual Meeting
An Idea whose Time has Come

It's time for another meeting! Where is it? Will I get there in time? What's the agenda?

Am I taking enough notes with me to the meeting? Will everyone else be able to make it? How will we keep the meeting on track?

And most importantly, what will I do if I get bored?!

If you find yourself asking these and other questions about meetings, it's time you took a good look at **Virtual Meeting (VM)**! **VM** combines all the hardware and software you need to hold your next meeting in Cyberspace, or as we here at **VM** refer to it - VirtualSpace. You can purchase the entire suite of **VM** or individual components to integrate with your existing hardware and software.

With **VM**, all meeting attendees are connected over the internet. With the Digital Mini-Cam on top of your PC (*that would now be a built-in webcam*), the Phone Headset and Internet Phone Software, it's like holding a tele-video conference, but much, much more! Now you don't have to go to meetings, they

In Search of a Right Brained Computer

can come to you, no matter how small your work area! **VM** also gives you the tools you need to hold an effective meeting! With the conference room designer software, the meeting facilitator can design the layout of the Virtual Conference Room, complete with tables, chairs, windows, and mood lights. As each attendee logs in, everyone will see them take his or her place at the table.

The Virtual Conference Room can also be set up as a lecture hall, complete with podium and lavaliere mic. If you find out everyone else has dressed up for this meeting, no problem, just click a button before you login and everyone else sees you in your best (or better), complete with Red Power Tie or Blazer.

The **VM** graphic artist's tablet allows you to simulate a white board discussion. Everyone can participate at the whiteboard. If you're a doodler, just click a button and the graphic artist's tablet becomes a doodle pad. You can save your doodles or erase them when you're done, just be sure to click the button before you start or you'll be doodling on the whiteboard, where everybody can see.

Need overheads, no problem with **VM**. Just click the slide-show button. Use the screen pen as a laser pointer. The slide show uses existing documents and graphics or those you create with **VM**'s own Docu-Graphi-Matic.

To make your meetings more effective, **VM** keeps track of the agenda right before your eyes. The meeting facilitator can tick off each agenda item as it's done. If you only need to attend part of the meeting, you can have **VM** notify you as soon as the previous item has been ticked off. **VM**'s Time Keeper notifies you if the time run's over on an agenda item. All attendees can immediately vote whether or not to continue this topic. Attendees can have weighted votes. The facilitator also has veto authority, and since it's now politically correct, line-item veto authority. **VM**'s Task Tracker Voice Recognition Software, can listen in on a discussion, and notify the attendees when it thinks they're getting off-track.

VM notifications can be set to red flashing lights, a screaming siren, or simply a Window's Message or a beep. Notifications can be set to any picture or sound you have on file or a combination.

In Search of a Right Brained Computer

This Intelligent Software can also tick off each agenda item, so the facilitator doesn't have to.

Need notes for the meeting? Just use **VM**'s Task Manager to switch to those notes. The conference room will remain in its own mini-window. To everyone else, it will look as though you just pulled them out of your briefcase and set them out on the table in front of you. You can also have **VM** import your notes for all to see.

And, finally, what to do if you get bored? Just click the right mouse button, and a whole list of options appears.

For starts, put Groucho Marx glasses on all the attendees.

Still bored, play 3D Tic-Tac-Toe on the Conference Whiteboard.

Let a mouse loose in the conference room and watch all the participants shriek and climb onto their chairs.

Put smiles on everyone.

Watch, as you take years and pounds off.

See everyone jump through the facilitator's hoops.

And if you're still bored, turn the Virtual Conference Room into a disco, complete with strobe lights and music.

Now, what's this? Everyone's attending an Hawaiian Luau instead. Or, while you're on the Internet, surf it! Or just surf some waves instead - who has time for golf anyway?

In Search of a Right Brained Computer

The Dance Partner

Right about now, you're probably thinking, "What about Macintoshes (Macs)? Aren't they right-brained?" Macs have some applications that right-brained people might use for music and art. Other computers can also use those types of applications. Apple computers might be more intuitive for right-brained people to use. But they still operate very linearly. They have trouble with interpreting close or nuances. And, they don't go with my shoes.

Google and other search engines have become very good at interpreting what you're searching for. Sometimes they interpret too well and search for something very different from what you thought you were asking. Guessing what you're meaning does not make a computer right-brained.

Still, applications for right-brained activities and allowing you to not have to state exactly what you mean in terms the computer can understand, are steps towards making a right-brained computer.

Let me explain it this way.

Computers were designed to solve mathematical equations. Express a problem as a mathematical equation and a computer can solve it. Besides being used to solve problems (as number crunchers), computers are used as highly advanced typewriters. Computers are also used to store information. Information is stored so that it can be retrieved later. The Internet connects several computers together, so that we can look up information that is stored on any of those computers. The Internet also allows us to communicate with others by means of the computer.

In all these interactions with a computer, we tell the computer what to do, and if we do it precisely and in the correct order, the computer will do exactly what it interprets that we told it to do. We tell the computer what to do step-by-step and it proceeds step-by-step (even if sometimes those

In Search of a Right Brained Computer

steps seem to be very large). A left-brained computer wants to know if a=b.

A right-brained computer is more of a dance partner than a slave. It understands your language and nuances, rather than you having to understand its language. It knows when you add a step, change a step, leave out a step; and when you change dance styles. A right-brained computer wants to know how much a is like b, where the degree and sort of likeness is defined by the user right this instant. A right-brained computer works in harmony with you, enhancing your work. A right-brained computer doesn't have to solve problems or accomplish anything. It can play and dabble. Though a right-brained computer could be used for business, it would understand the world of non-business – the world of sharing, friendship, and play.

> *Having Games and Social Sharing Apps like Facebook or Email on your computer does not make it right-brained. However, those Apps might help you perform right-brained activities.*

A right-brained computer would help right-brained people do what right-brained people do best. It would help them play and sing and compose music, dance and choreograph, draw and paint, write prose and

In Search of a Right Brained Computer

poetry, use and create patterns and textures and colors, act and write plays and direct movies, meditate and pray, and see the big picture.

The ideal right-brained computer would be aesthetic and pleasing to the eye. A right-brained computer would allow you to set the tempo and rhythm. A right-brained computer would move the way you do. It would interact with all of your senses, rather than just with one or two of them.

> *Computers which have a touch screen with a stylus or pen are more right-brained than those which don't.*
>
> *My computer has a touch screen and stylus. Being left-brained, I rarely use them.*

A right-brained computer would be consistent, but would not make you be consistent. That is, it would be consistent until you decided you wanted it to be consistent in a different manner, which might be being consistently random. A right-brained computer would reason the way you reason at any point in time. It would be able to see similarities between things, the way you see similarities between things.

In Search of a Right Brained Computer

A right-brained computer would be inclusive enough that even those who are left-brained could use it in the way they want. People are not usually only right-brained or only left-brained. People do some activities more right-brained. For others, they use a left-brained approach. So, a right-brained computer would let a person choose the level of right-brainedness they wanted to use at any given time.

At least that's what my right-brained wife Terry tells me.

My approach to making a right-brained computer, would be to simplify a left-brained computer; add functionality that allows a computer to be a dance partner, and then add activities that right-brained people would do – music, art, drama, etc.

I've been making computers simpler for everyone for over 40 years. Making computers simpler, makes them easier for both left-brained and right-brained people to use. Simple is good, but simple is not right-brained. Simple to use left-brained computers are still left-brained computers. They are not dance partners.

Adding right-brained functionality to a left-brained computer may not be the easiest thing in the world. It may be easier to start from scratch and design a right-brained computer and then add left-brained functionality; or start from scratch and design a totally right-brained computer.

If right-brained functionality were added to a left-brained computer, would it truly be right-brained functionality and reasoning, or would it still have a distinctively left-brained finger print to it? We will probably not be able to answer that question until we have right-brained people using right-brained computers.

It may be, that like ourselves, in order for a computer to perform in both a left-brained and a right-brained manner, a computer will actually need two separate yet communicating parts or hemispheres.

In Search of a Right Brained Computer

I tend to approach everything computer-related from a left-brained way of thinking. So, in my search for a right-brained computer, I will continue to seek input from my right-brained wife and others who are more right-brained than I.

Likewise, building the ideal computer may require both left-brained and right-brained people working together — what a concept!

In Search of a Right Brained Computer

Terry Two

A Simple, Consistent, and Powerful Approach to Computers

Introduction

Imagine what it would be like if your computer was easy to use. Imagine, that instead of remembering how 10 apps or more worked, you only had to remember how one app worked. Imagine being able to find everything on your computer easily.

Imagine that your computer is named Terry Two and that your screen always looks pretty much the same. Your screen looks something like this.

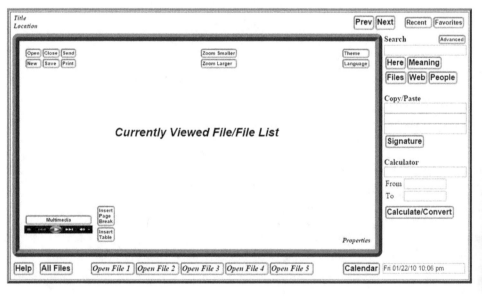

In Search of a Right Brained Computer

Terry Two is my first attempt at designing a computer for right-brain people. It's a nice first step, but is not yet a right-brained computer. It is simple and consistent. It is also powerful enough to do everything normal computers can do. But it will need to grow up to become a right-brained computer. I'll discuss that in a later section of the book. For now, Terry Two is easier for everybody to learn and use. As Terry Two grows up and becomes right-brained, it will keep the consistency and ease it learned as a youth. As it grows up, right-brained functionality will be added until it truly becomes a right-brained computer.

Terry Two has one view, picture, or basic screen layout for everything you view. I'll describe Terry Two by going through each item in the view. This view is shown on the previous page.

Navigation

➔ Starting across the top of the view

Title – The title is the title of the file. For many files, the Title is the File Name.

Location – The location tells where the file is located. If the file is a webpage, the location is the URL or link to that webpage. If the file is on a computer, the location is the path and file name. You can rename the file by changing the file name part of the location. For example, location might be *http://www.google.com/* or *Libraries\Documents\Terry Two*.

In Search of a Right Brained Computer

Prev/Next – The Prev and Next button take you to the previous or next open file. This is the same as the back and forward buttons on a web browser, but it applies to any open file (webpage or other).

Recent/Favorites – The Recent and Favorites buttons both display a list of files in the area below these buttons and above the clock. When a list of files is displayed here, the other items in this area are hidden. Recent displays the recent files you've viewed. You can limit the list to webpages, websites, or other files. Favorites displays the files you view most often.

In Search of a Right Brained Computer

Tools

→ Continuing down the right-hand side of the view
Search – Enter the word or phrase you want to search
for in the box. To search for something in the current
view, click the Here button. To search for definitions,
synonyms, quotes, translations, etc. about the word or
phrase; click the Meaning button. To search all files,
click the Files button. To search the web, click the Web
button. To search for People, click the People button.

For more search options click the Advanced button.
Advanced options include finding only exact matches,
finding only matches which match the case
(upper/lower) of what you entered, and finding only
whole words (when searching for "the" only "the" is
found, not "their"). The Advanced options also include a
Replace With box. If you want to replace the text in the Search box with
something else, enter the replacement text in the Replace With box.

The advanced options show below the search buttons and above the
clock, covering other items in the Tools area of the screen.

Copy/Paste – The copy/paste area gives you three boxes for
copying/pasting. To copy something, select it and drag it to one of these
boxes. To paste it, drag it from the box to where you want it pasted. The
something can be anything you can select – text, file, etc. Once you've
dragged something into the box, the box shows you what is contained in it
– the text, file name, or title. When you paste something, you are asked if
you want to delete the original. If you are copying/pasting text in the view,
you can simply select it and drag it to the new location, without sticking it
in the copy/paste boxes.

Dale Stubbart

In Search of a Right Brained Computer

The Signature button allows you to edit/paste your signature or salutation. To edit your signature, click the Signature button. Your signature is shown in the area below the Signature button and above the clock. To paste or insert your signature, drag the Signature button to where you want to paste your signature.

Calculator – The Calculator area allows you to perform simple calculations. Just enter the numbers in the box and press the operator keys (+,-,*,/,=) and you will see the result in the box. This works just like most calculators, except the number and operator buttons are not shown.

To convert from one unit of measure to another, enter the from unit in the From box. Enter the to unit in the To box. Then click the Convert button.

Clock and Calendar – The clock displays the current time. Since the time is synchronized with the master clock and formatted according to the normal format of the country you are in, there is no need to change it. However, if you want to change it, change the format, or display the time for a different time zone, place your cursor in the clock box and right-click to access these features.

Right-clicking anywhere gives you access to common tasks associated with the area your cursor is in. Most of the common tasks are available without right-clicking. You only need to right-click for advanced features. Advanced features are not always documented, so if you're curious, place your cursor somewhere in the view and right-click.

Click the Calendar button to open the calendar. The Calendar is displayed in the Current View area. Once the Calendar is open, you can add events, tasks, and reminders.

In Search of a Right Brained Computer

Current View Area

➜ The rest of the view

Open – The Open button opens a file. Select the file you want to open, then click the Open button. If a file is currently selected, it will be opened. If not, select one and that file will be opened. After the file is opened, the Current View shows the contents of that file and the file name or title becomes an Open File button.

New – The New button opens a new, empty file. You can give the file a title and name now, or when you save/close the file. To give the file a title now, type the title into the Title area. As you type the title, it is filled in as the file name. You can give the file a name which is different from the title, by typing that name into the file name area of the Location area.
 Enter the contents of the file in the Current View area.

In Search of a
Right Brained
Computer

Close – The Close button closes the current file. If any changes have been made since the last time you saved the file, you are asked whether you want to save those changes or not. When the file is closed, the file contents of the open file which was viewed most recently are shown. If there are no other open files, all files are shown.

Save – The Save button saves changes to the currently viewed file. If the file name is the same as that of another file in the same location, you are asked if you want to replace the other file with this file. If you answer no, you can save the file in another location or change the name of the currently open file or the name of the other file.

In Search of a Right Brained Computer

To:	Reply		
Copy:			
Hidden Copy:			Send It!

Send – The Send button sends the currently viewed or currently selected file (if viewing all files) to somebody via email. To, Copy, and Hidden Copy buttons and boxes are shown in the Current View area. Enter the names or email addresses of the people you are sending the file to, in the appropriate boxes. If you need to look up the name or email address, click on the To, Copy, or Hidden Copy button, to select people from among all your contacts. To send a reply back to the person who sent you this email, click Reply (rather than To). This will fill in the name of the person who sent the email, plus the names of all the people that person sent the email to. You can remove any names you don't want the email sent to before clicking OK.

Print – The Print button prints the currently viewed or currently selected file. A preview of how the file will look when it is printed is displayed. You can remove pages from being printed or portions of a page. You can rearrange the contents of the file and space them the way you want. You can change page sizes and margins. You can add a Page Header (often contains Title or File Name) and a Page Footer (often contains Author, Date, Page Number and Number of Pages).

Once you have the preview looking the way you want to, you can save these settings.

Then you can specify the Number of Copies and Print Quality.

In Search of a Right Brained Computer

Zoom Smaller/Zoom Larger – Click these buttons to view whatever's in the Current View area at a smaller or larger size.

Theme – Clicking the Theme button displays Theme or formatting tools in the area below the Language button and above Properties.

A theme coordinates elements on your document, so that they are well-coordinated, aesthetically speaking. Theme elements are colors, fonts and font sizes. The Theme Bar makes it easy to set a theme for this document; switch themes; use different theme elements; and modify, create, delete, and rename themes.

Features you can set with theme tools include the background, borders, fonts, and alignment (spacing).

Language – Clicking the Language button displays Language tools in the area below the Language button and above Properties.

Tools on the language bar include translation, spelling and grammar checking, and access to special characters, symbols, diacritic marks (including accent marks), and emoticons. Language tools also give you access to texting abbreviations and allows you to type in word mode, rather than character mode. Word mode allows you to enter a few characters for common words, rather than all the characters.

Multimedia – Clicking the Multimedia button displays tools for editing multimedia files or the multimedia contents of a file. These tools are displayed in the area above the Multimedia button. Multimedia tools include those for editing pictures, sounds, and movies.

In Search of a Right Brained Computer

Picture editing tools include drawing tools – pencil, brush, paint can, eraser, line, box, oval, callout, etc. Picture editing tools also allow you to adjust the picture and add special features, borders, and masks.

Sound editing tools allow you to adjust the volume, length, quality, and voice of the sound.

Movie editing tools allow you to edit frames of a movie and the transition between frames.

The Multimedia Control bar below the Multimedia button allows you to play the current movie or sound and adjust the volume.

Insert Page Break – Clicking the Insert Page Break button, inserts a page break at the current cursor location. You can also insert page breaks after clicking the Print button, while you're previewing the print.

Insert Table – Inserts a table at the current cursor location. You can enter text, numbers, and formulas in the table. When you are working in a table, Table tools are displayed in the area above the Multimedia button. Table tools allow you to insert or delete rows and columns. They also help you with formulas. To change the border of a table, click on the Theme button to get access to border and other theme tools.

Properties – The Properties area shows properties of the currently viewed or currently selected file. This information may include file size, number of words, number of characters, display size of a picture, current cursor location, and other items of interest.

In Search of a
Right Brained
Computer

Current View Contents

➔ The bottom of the view

➔ Current View buttons

| Help | All Files | | Open File 1 | Open File 2 | Open File 3 | Open File 4 | Open File 5 |

Help – The Help button displays help. Help is displayed that pertains to the area of the screen where your cursor is. So, if you'd like help with units of measure, place the cursor in either the From or To box in the Calculator area, and press the Help button. The Help contents are displayed in the Current View area.

All Files – Clicking the All Files button displays all files in the Current View area. This will be explained in more detail later. Basically it shows you files, rather than the contents of a particular file.

Open File ... – As each file is opened, its name or title is displayed in this area as a button. The contents of that open file are shown in the Current View area. To switch between open files, click on the appropriate Open File button.

In Search of a Right Brained Computer

Files

➔ Current View area

The Current View area shows the contents of currently open file, or all files.

When the contents of a file are shown here, you can edit, arrange, and lay them out the way you want. Sometimes it is easier to leave the layout until you're previewing the Print.

All Files are viewed as a File Cabinet. The area below the Language button shows tools for working with files. These tools help you navigate among the files, organize them, and view them as you wish. You can view the files in summary or detail mode. You can view mini pictures of picture and movie files and snippets of other files.

You can view only a group of files, filtering the list. One group is files you have received or sent (email files). To limit the files to those containing only a certain word or phrase, enter that word or phrase into the Search box and click Files.

To copy a file, drag it to a copy box.

In Search of a Right Brained Computer

Title	Subject	Received	Priority
From	1st Line	Action	Rule
Title	Subject	Received	Priority
From	1st Line	Action	Rule
Title	Subject	Received	Priority
From	1st Line	Action	Rule

The view of email files, shows the title/subject of each email, who it is from, the first two lines of the email, when it was received, any action you have set for the email, the priority of the email and any rule which affects this email.

Emails are organized by Priority, Action Date & Time, and Received Date & Time. You can change this order with the File tools in the area below the Language button.

To add the Sender (From) to your contacts, drag the From Contents to the Search box, and click People. If this person is not already in your contacts, you will then be given a chance to add them.

You can change the action by placing the cursor in the Action area. You will be asked to choose an action or enter you own. You are also asked to enter a date and time for the action. Actions include, Follow Up, Expire, Change Priority, etc. Actions in the Action area are those that are set to happen at a certain time.

You can change the Priority, by entering a new Priority – High, Medium, or Low.

In Search of a Right Brained Computer

You can change (or add) a rule, by placing the cursor in the Rule area. Options to create a rule are shown in the area below the Language button. Rules include rating the Sender or content as spam, and automatically setting an action or priority based on Sender or content.

In Search of a Right Brained Computer

Security

To turn Terry Two on or off, flip the on/off switch. When you turn Terry Two on, the view or basic screen layout is shown. The Current View area contains entry boxes for your Username and Password. After you have entered these (signed in), you are given a chance to change security before continuing with your other work.

Security information is shown in the Current View area. You can change your Username or Password. You can add a Security Question in case you forget your password. If you have authority to do so, you can add other users to this computer and set Parental Control levels.

To switch users, turn Terry Two off and back on.

When you turn Terry Two off, you are given a chance to save any changes you have made. When you sign into Terry Two again, any files you previously had open are open to where they were open when you signed off.

Terry Two allows you to do complex tasks through a simple interface. This allows you to do more in a shorter period of time, so you won't need to be spend so much time in front a computer screen.

In Search of a Right Brained Computer

Ok, ready for another break? Thought so.

On Hold to Music
An Idea whose Time has Come

OnHold TM (OHTM) stands for "On Hold To Music", and it could change your whole attitude to being put on hold.

This is the scenario: You call up a company, like say OHTM, for example. You are greeted by a friendly person who says, "Hello. This is OHTM. Can I put you on hold?" Without thinking, you respond, "Sure". You're immediately put on hold and think, "Now why did I do that for? I promised myself, I'd always reply NO to that question."

Then comes the pleasant surprise. A recording, with a pleasant voice of the opposite sex, says "Please press your listening preference." You hear one part of your mind say, "Why, You of course, Honey." The recording continues: "Or press # for a menu."

Being a newcomer to this, you press #. The recording continues, "Please press 1 to hear special announcements about OHTM. Please press 2 for automated Help. Press 3 for Rock and Roll. 4 for Classical. 5 for Jazz. 6 for Country. 7 for Oldies but Goodies. 8 for a Talk Show. 9 for Muzac. * for Silence. And as always, press # for this menu."

You are tempted for a second to continue listening to this lovely voice, and just keep pressing #; but only for a minute. Unfortunately today you

In Search of a Right Brained Computer

have lots of work to get done, so you press * for Silence. Some other day you'll listen to your favorite music or to OHTM's special announcements; or maybe even, no don't even think about pressing #!

In Search of a Right Brained Computer

Is Terry Two Right-Brained?

Let's see how close we've come to having a right-brained computer.

Questions	Left-Brained	Right-Brained
Story	Present-State	History & Purpose
Usability	Control	What does it do for me?
Sensory	Look	Appearance
Value	Cost	Worth
Life	Lifetime	Legacy
Communication	Information	Life
Need/Want	I need this for	This makes me complete

Story: Terry Two has a history. Her purpose is to eventually become the ultimate right-brained computer, but be flexible enough that left-brained users will enjoy working with her.

Usability: Terry Two makes it simple to see what she will do for you – keep track of documents and emails and allow you to change them simply. Not much right-brained stuff there, but music, art, etc applications can be built to use that simple layout. Still, simple is not right-brained.

Sensory: The appearance hasn't really been broached, but it should look sleek and elegant. It should also look stylish and be able to change colors to go with any outfit. It will need a good sound system for my auditory senses.

In Search of a Right Brained Computer

Value: Terry Two will hold a lot of worth, if you don't have to strain to think the way she does (because she thinks the way you do). Her worth is that when you need to use the computer, it actually speeds things up, rather than slowing you down.

Life: For Terry Two to have a legacy, she must be built sustainably with easily replaceable parts. Things must be clearly labeled or at least there should be a cheat sheet on the back. The parts that are replaced will need to be easily convertible into some other product, so that they have a second life. And she must be easily upgradeable, extending her life.

Her ultimate legacy will be that she left no humans behind because they didn't think the way she did.

Communication: Current social apps communicate more of life than information. But often, they do not communicate it well. That's because they just let us communicate the way we communicate, which sometimes is just a bunch of gobbledygook – unintelligible at best. If Terry Two is to improve on that, she must help us communicate better or at least turn our gobbledygook into intelligent blather.

Need/Want: If Terry Two fits simply into our lives, then there's a chance that she might make us more complete.

So, Terry Two has a long way to go, but hopefully, I've provided enough inspiration and direction for somebody else to complete this project.

In Search of a Right Brained Computer

My brain really hurts now thinking about all this right-brained stuff. I'm going to have to spend an entire day, reading programming manuals.

If your brain is hurting, it might be time for another break.

The Ergomnible MiceBoard
An Idea whose Time has come

The **Ergomnible MiceBoard (EM)** combines the best of keyboards and mice into one complete design. **Ergo** because it's ergonomical. **Omni** because it can be and do just about anything. The **EM** is so advanced, it comes with its own software. The **EM** uses infrared technology so cables don't get in your way (*now that would be bluetooth technology*).

To design the **EM**, we started with the standard 101 keyboard. (104 keyboard users read on.) Then we removed everything to the right of the main keyboard. We used memory plastic (the same thing that's used in glasses frames), to allow it to become a wave keyboard, or a standard keyboard. Pneumatic lifts at the back of the keyboard, let it tilt as much or as little as you desire. We split the keyboard in half, much like the common wave design, but the two pieces can be placed as far or as near apart as you like, even together.

Then we put it on wheels, and gave it brakes, so that when you need to move the keyboard (either half or both), you can do so. Finally, we gave each key an LED display.

In Search of a Right Brained Computer

Now, using the included software, you can download fonts from your software to your keyboard. You can also set up your keyboard with the QWERTY or DVORAK style, or any style you like. All these functions are controlled by the included software or by extra buttons above the function keys. (You always wondered why there was all that wasted space.)

Then we took the numeric key pad, and made two of them - one for each hand. These are usually placed on each side of the main keyboard, but you can place them wherever you like.

We placed the three control keys that are usually above the cursor keys above the numeric key pad instead. The lights were placed above the main keyboard where you're more likely to see them.

As for the cursor keys, Page Up, Page Down, etc., they can be accessed by turning off Num Lock, so we removed them altogether. With two numeric keypads, you can use one for cursors and the other for numbers – your choice. The numeric keypad is also made of memory plastic and can assume a wave or standard format.

The tilt and wheel features are also included on the numeric key pad as are the download capabilities.

By now, you're probably thinking, this **EM** has some neat features, but they've taken away lots of other features I enjoy on a daily basis. Is it worth the switch? Now, let us introduce you to the best feature of the **EM**. The mice.

In Search of a Right Brained Computer

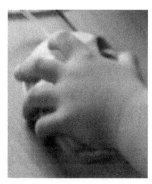

That's right, the **EM** comes with two mice - one for each hand.

And because we want the **EM** to be the best experience you've had in a while, it comes with its own mice pads which are thick, plush, and large.

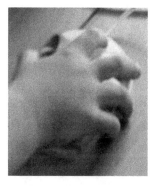

If you're limited on workspace, don't consider a different keyboard and mouse, get more workspace or read on. Each mouse uses a unique five-button design. Using Memory Plastic, the mouse conforms to the shape of your hand, from Petite to Globe-Trotter size. Each of the eight finger buttons is programmable. So, if you're missing the extra 104 keyboard keys and cursor keys, just program them into finger buttons.

The thumb buttons can be pressed, but they can also be slid in any of four directions. (There's a reason people have opposable thumbs.) The press of the thumb buttons can be programmed. Slide the thumb button to switch the finger buttons (and thumb press) of that hand to a different set of functions, which is also programmable.

So each mouse has five different buttons, which can each perform five different functions. That's a total of 50 functions. But that's not all. You can also press mice buttons in combination, and all the combinations are programmable. That's so many combinations, we'll let you figure it out! Suffice it to say that it's enough buttons to eliminate your need for the main keyboard and numeric key pads.

In Search of a
Right Brained
Computer

Using our buttoning course, you can quickly learn how to enter all the information you need, just using the mice. After all, aren't you tired of having your hands jump all over the place from keyboard to mouse and back?

And eliminating the time it takes to move your hands around, could mean you'll be entering information even faster than before. And it will certainly eliminate your worrying over how to reach the 6 key on the main keyboard!